FEED THE BEAST

Pádraig Ó Tuama is a poet and theologian from Ireland. His work has appeared in *Poetry Ireland, The Harvard Review, Gutter* and the *Academy of American Poets*, as well as being featured on national broadcasters in Ireland, the USA, Australia, the UK and New Zealand. His podcast *Poetry Unbound* from On Being Studios has been downloaded over six million times, the compnion book *Poetry Unbound* is available from Canongate/WW Norton.

Also by Pádraig Ó Tuama

Contents

ISBN: 978-1-915079-52-7

Cover designed by Aaron Kent

Edited & Typeset by Aaron Kent

Broken Sleep Books Ltd
Rhydwen
Talgarreg
Ceredigion
SA44 4HB

Broken Sleep Books Ltd
Fair View
St Georges Road
Cornwall
PL26 7YH

Feed the Beast

Pádraig Ó Tuama

Jackals shall meet with monsters,
goat-demons shall call to each other;
there too Lilith shall repose,
and find a place to rest.
— The book of Isaiah, chapter 34

The Butcher of Eden

Now God made Adam and Eve coats of skins and dressed them.
— Genesis 3:21

And when he was finished,
he scraped fat
from the backs of stretched skins,
wiped the blood,
sewed the seams,
bit the thread with teeth
and said:
Dress yourselves in these.

And they said:
what is this verb?

God shoved his knife into the earth, and said:
It's like make believe
but for your body.

They looked at all the meat
still steaming
from when it was alive.

God said: Eat.
And watched while
beasts of Eden fed
on beasts of Eden.

Let the Waters Swarm with a Swarm of Living Beings

I've been swimming round here for a while now
and while I've never touched the ocean floor,
I've tried.

You notice things out here. The way the wind
makes waves chop at odd angles, the way the water feels
warmer at the top,

the way the moon makes music when you're half dead
with cold, the ways of frozen bones, the way the morning
never feels the same.

Once a seal bumped me. Came right up to me
like a sea puppy and — I swear — it smiled. I was floating happy
after that. I said

the ocean was my home. Then the storm came.
Then the waves. Then the lightning spiked the surface. Thunder
clapped. Hungry beasts swam round me. I saw seagulls eyeing me for scraps.

Seven Deadly Sonnets

> And some deep prayers were shaped like sonnets
> — *Patrick Kavanagh*

(i)   The Exorcism

I wished you weren't American. I wished you didn't see
intrinsic evil in me. I wished you hadn't dragged
my secret from me. Now I know you knew already,
someone squealed. I wished you didn't put your hands on me
while you were screaming at the devils in me, all my
homosexualities. I wished you'd never gathered
people round, instructing them to pray in tongues,
or read from Revelations, or chant JESUS.JESUS.JESUS.
I wished you'd shut up. I repeated jesusjesusjesus.
I wished he'd answered. I wished you dead.

And I was frightened at the violence in me, and the
nest of demons in me, I wondered where they lived:
in my semen? in the dreams I had of being kissed?
Why did they breed in me? My God. My Exorcist.

> 'Have you come to destroy us?
> I know who you are, the Holy One of God.'
> But Jesus rebuked him, saying,
> "Be muzzled and come out of him."
> — *The Gospel of Mark, chapter one.*

(ii)   The Exorcism

You	have a devil in you.
You	have destruction. You have rot in
You.	You can't give in to
Your	abominable behaviour, your rejection of

Your	nature, Your denial of y
our	manhood and
Your	hatred of the order of creation.
Your	body's made for other things than that.

You	must stop thinking of men's bodies in the way we think
You	think about men's bodies. We'll fuck
You	in the ass if we catch you at that again. We hear it makes
You	bleed.

Gather round our burdened brother, brothers. Bless him. Hunt the
devil from him. Place your hands upon his shoulders, let us pray.

If a man lies with a male
as with a woman,
both of them have committed
an abomination;
they shall be put to death;
their blood is upon them.
— *The Book of Leviticus, chapter twenty.*

(iii)   The Exorcism

The way to break a man is to make him hate
himself. So I found myself at doorways: one at the top

steps where my exorcisers waited; getting absolution
from a priest who thrust his crotch into my face; shaking

outside a bar I was too chaste to enter; & now this empty
room. Divide and conquer works for countries. People too.

The exorcisers said my sexuality would change if I Called
Down my Authority In Jesus. A prize for true believers. So they

emptied out a room where I could cast out all my devils by my
self. *Till what's inside of you's outside of you.* I locked the door,

prayed harder than I'd prayed before. Stayed an hour. When I came out
saying I was still unfree, they said I was beyond their powers,

but they'd heard about a man who knew psychology. A trusted Christian
man who'd cure me. He'd make me. Truly. Finally. Manly.

at the entrance is sin, a crouching-demon,
toward you his lust—
but you can rule over him.
— *The Book of Genesis, chapter four.*

13

(iv)   Adam & Eve not Adam & Steve

I buy the book that maps out the five types of homosexual.
Which one's me?

All five types needy, male,
all five types failures.

How did my struggle start? In a garden?
In the sibilants of a serpent?

Was I spanked too little? Or too much?
Was it school? Or sport? I'm can't kick straight. That's it.

The book says my desires are just urges to consume the thing I'm not,
that my lust for cock makes me a cannibal.

I share my secret with a man who wants to be my mentor.
We arrange to meet twice weekly for accountability and once

after a chat where he'd asked about abuse, he grabs my balls and
slaps my ass. He laughs it off, says *all straight lads do this*.

> All will be purged with fire,
> and the fire will test.
> — *The first letter to the Corinthians, chapter three.*

(v)   Volta

After Shakespeare, Sonnet 130

My exorciser's eyes were nothing like the sun,
they had no fire. If twisted be the language
bad priests speak, his tongue was like a
lyre, sweeter than the eucharist. If hate be

harsh, why then his actions felt more tender
than a father's. I have heard the furious from
the pulpit. This man's work was quiet as abuse. I loved
the promises he made, they wound around my

heart with knots of wonder. I have heard of charlatans
who charge, I swear he would have paid me
for my custom. His rates were reasonable and his
burden subtle. Some terrorise. He Christianised.

I swear to you his heaven rhymed with hell.
I know he'll claw his way to glory. Me as well.

Lord, do you want us
to command fire
to come down from heaven
to consume them?
— *The Gospel of Luke, chapter nine.*

(vi)   Hate the Sin and Hate the Sinner

It's all in the way you use your language, he said.
Same Sex Attraction's a burden you don't need to bear.
That's why I'm here for you. To help you.
Repeat after me: "I'm not gay. Just broken."

He told me my past would need to be redeemed
by Jesus. *You don't need deliverance*, he said,
just healing. Take off your anorak. Relax.

It began to end when I wouldn't go along
with the homework he prescribed.
He'd told me to pick the type of girl I'd choose
when I was cured. *You're strong*, he said.
Nice back. They like that. Tell me what you'd do.

I refused. His anger flashed. *You don't know what I do for you,*
he said. *You need more Submission. Lordship. Truth.*

As the tongue of fire
devours the stubble,
so their root will become rotten,
and their blossom go up like dust.
— *The Book of Isaiah, chapter five.*

(vii)   O What A Marvel It Appeared To Me

I knew it was him as soon as I saw him.
He saw me too.

I was curious if he'd changed —
I like to believe people do, eventually.

Ten years since he'd made me
account for what he called
homosexual erections
in weekly sessions he called therapy.

I've got plenty of obsessions,
but he's not one of them anymore.
All it took was time and safety. Five years? Twenty?

I don't know how I made it through.

When I saw him, I gave him what he said God gave me.
Silence. Opportunity.

> Oh quanto parve a me gran maraviglia
> O what a marvel it appeared to me
> — *Dante, Inferno. Canto XXXIV. trans: Longfellow, 1867*

what
kind of prayer could ever be trusted without
evidence of a free tongue?
— *No'u Revilla*

Feed the Beast

Back when I believed God would speak to me
God spoke to me,

and asked me who
I thought I was keeping happy.

I was keeping a six day fast,
feeding on fat and faith and failure,

and one evening, praying instead of eating,
worshipping what I did not know,

What I Did Not Know spoke to me
telling me to feed my hunger.

I was seventeen, or twenty, or forty five, or nine
and zeal was eating me alive.

When I heard the voice, I was sitting the ground,
wrapped around an instrument.

I had rid the room of imagery
believing that reading and not eating would be enough.

There was the sound of my stomach growling.
And the sound of nails scratching strings on a guitar.

There was the sound of whatever
made that starving beast start feeling.

There is a Time to Love and a Time to Hate; a Time for Making War

— The book of Ecclesiastes, Chapter 3, v 8

Responsum of the Congregation for the Doctrine of the Faith to a dubium regarding the blessing of the unions of persons of the same sex

TO THE QUESTION PROPOSED:
Does the Church have the power to give the blessing to unions of persons of the same sex?
RESPONSE: Negative.

Explanatory Note:
Therefore, only those realities which are in themselves ordered to serve those ends are congruent with the essence of the blessing imparted by the Church.
For this reason, it is not licit to impart a blessing on relationships, or partnerships, even stable, that involve sexual activity outside of marriage (i.e., outside the indissoluble union of a man and a woman open in itself to the transmission of life), as is the case of the unions between persons of the same sex. The presence in such relationships of positive elements, which are in themselves to be valued and appreciated, cannot justify these relationships and render them legitimate objects of an ecclesial blessing, since the positive elements exist within the context of a union not ordered to the Creator's plan.

Furthermore, since blessings on **persons** are **in** relationship with the sacraments, the blessing of **homosexual unions** cannot be considered licit. This is because they would **constitute** a certain imitation or analogue of the nuptial blessing invoked on the man and woman united in the sacrament of Matrimony, while in fact "there are absolutely no grounds for considering homosexual unions to be in any way similar or even remotely analogous to God's plan for marriage and **family**".

The declaration of the unlawfulness of blessings of unions between persons of the same sex is not therefore, and is not intended to be, a form of unjust discrimination, but rather a reminder of the truth of the liturgical rite and of the very nature of the sacramentals, as the Church understands them.

The **Christian** community and its **Pastors are called to** welcome with respect and sensitivity persons with homosexual inclinations, and will know how to find the most appropriate ways, consistent with Church teaching, to proclaim to them the Gospel in its fullness. At the same time, they should recognize the genuine nearness of the Church – which **p**rays for th**e**m, accompa**n**ies **t**hem **an**d shares their journey of Christian faith – and receive the teachings with sin**ce**re openness.

The answer to the proposed dubium does not preclude the blessings given to individual **persons with homosexual inclinations,** who manifest the will to live in fidelity to the revealed plans of God as proposed by Church teaching. Rather, it **declares illicit any form of** blessing that tends to acknowledge their unions as such. In this case, in fact, the blessing would manifest not the intention to entrust such individual persons to the protection and help of **God,** in the sense mentioned above, but to approve and encourage a choice and a way of life **that cannot be recognized as** objectively ordered to the revealed plans of **God.**

At the same time, the Church recalls that **God** Himself never ceases to bless each of His **pilgrim** children in this world, because for Him "we are more important to God than all of the sins that we can commit".

But he does not and cannot bless sin: he blesses sinful man, so that he may recognize that he is part of his plan of love and allow himself to be changed by him. He in fact "takes us as we are, but never leaves us as we are". For the **above** mentioned reasons, **the Church** does not have, and cannot have, the power to bless unions of persons of the same sex in the sense intended above. The Sovereign Pontiff Francis, at the Audience granted to the undersigned Secretary of this Congregation, was informed and gave his assent to **the** publication of the above-mentioned Responsum ad dubium, with the annexed Explanatory Note. Rome, from the Offices of the Congregation for the Doctrine of the Faith, the 22nd of February 2021, **Feast** of the Chair **of** Saint Peter, Apostle. Luis F. Card. Ladaria, S.I. Prefect ✠ Giacomo Morandi Archbishop tit. of Cerveteri Secretary [1] FRANCIS, Apostolic Exhortation Amoris laetitia, 250. [2] SYNOD OF BISHOPS, Final Document of the XV Ordinary General Assembly, 150. [3] SECOND VATICAN ECUMENICAL COUNCIL, Constitution on the Sacred Liturgy Sacrosanctum Concilium, 60. [4] RITUALE ROMANUM ex Decreto Sacrosancti Oecumenici Concilii Vaticani II instauratum auctoritate Ioannis Pauli PP. II promulgatum, De bendictionibus, Praenotanda Generalia, n.9. [5] Ibidem, n. 10. [6] Catechism of the Catholic Church, 2357. [7] In fact, the nuptial blessing refers back to the creation account, in which **God**'s blessing on man and woman is related.

A Man Shall Lie With A Man

I've got nothing to be ashamed of
in the manhood department
if you know what I mean, he said,
grabbing flesh inside his jeans.

We were standing round a barbecue
cooking meat we hadn't beaten to death,
and the talk had turned to manhood
so the man had turned to size.

Of course it was met with laughter
and some banter about sausage
but then the talk turned to virtue
and the measure of a man:

his love for his family; his love for his wife;
his prayer life; his temptations;
his resistance to temptations; his provision;
his love for his God who had created him.

And then one man named a grief,
and another named a vice.
One man asked for prayers for consolation.
One man phoned his wife.

We pitched tents and unpacked bags,
pissed beer and tea into flowing streams,
lay down with each other under canvas, warmed
by feathers and each other's heat.

Not Drowning, Burning

кому суждено утонуть, не сгорит

Dance like everybody's watching, he said,
otherwise what's the point? Then he rattled
off some proverb in Russian
and told me to guess the meaning.

He whispered it in my ear again.
Feeling flirty, I guessed something about
undressing, but he laughed said *No!* said
Those destined to burn will never drown.

Later, when he made moves to get me horizontal,
I was all lit up with shame. He stopped, said
Let's warm up. And then he kissed me.
Not all men are so kind when let down.

We wound our way to an all night teashop
and he whistled harmonies to Tchaikovsky
while I looked around for anything to keep me going.
Him fluent. He flaring. Him fluid. Me fire.

The Underneath

The underneath. That was the first devil. It was always with me.

— Marie Howe

Here's the thing:

underneath the rage, the hurt,
underneath the hurt, the expectation,
underneath the expectation is hope in a something
underneath the hope there's hunger
underneath the hunger, a deeper hunger still.

I wake to an old story, and repeat it in the shower,
repeat it over tea, repeat it, amplify it,
put books into a bag, start up the car
and wait for the windows to de-mist,
I think about it at the junction, at the lights,
at the intersection, at the place where idiots make the same mistake
they always make while ignoring all the lanes placed there
to make us safe.

And underneath the story is a story,
underneath that story there is time,
underneath all time is memory,
and underneath all memory is a future and its questions.

I'm seized by an old dream. In it, I'm at speed,
but I'm not driving, no-one is. I'm on a train, an old one,
going underground. And I know I need to jump. I can see and I can't see
at all, there is wind and dark and terrible velocity, I know
that if I jump, I might die. I know that if I don't, I will not
survive.

Underneath desire is a hope to keep on living,
underneath the hope to keep on living is loss,
underneath the loss is my desperation for acceptance,

underneath that desperation is the belief that I am hateable,
underneath all that is fury and underneath the fury
is the hunter. Underneath the hunter is the hunt.

Notes on Righteousness

Even if you slay me, I will still argue.
— *The Book of Job.*

Everybody told me I was wrong
but something in me
said I wasn't.

/

If I am mistaken
even if God lays down
his pen and shuts the book

I'll still have my say.

/

If I am correct
then erect me
like an evergreen.

/

You can suffer in sulphur.
You can wander far from mapped land
and still find a way to say
the things that others say are
unsayable.

/

Feed me

/

Do you know men who still wrap
themselves around themselves
at night?

Many of us
sleep like this.

xx

/

When the devil, dressed in velvet,
slid near me,
he whispered to me
with his silky tongue.

I hung my head
and stared down at my body,
hummed a tune of shame.
He slipped away.

/

One God went to grow.
Grow a congregation.
One God and God's rabid dog
went to grow a congregation.

Three Gods went to grow
Grow a congregation
Three Gods, Two Gods, One God and God's rabid dog
went to grow a congregation.

/

Did you know that *mega*
comes from *meh*
comes from मह
meaning sacrifice?

How many sacrifices are made in the pursuit
of greatness?

/

If You want me
You can find me
down where Your
light dims.

Here, I can breathe
and smell old trees.
Here there's
turf and fire.

/

Someone

Someone gets up after sex

and doesn't cough up

shame

like phlegm.

Someone.

Someone

else.

Out

After I left the job
with the friends
who said they'd
treat me with compassion
if I fell,
an old friend asked me
what I wanted
with my future.

Sex and bit more money,
I said,
sipping on a coffee
in a café on a Sunday morning.

Ha! My old friend's laughter
was a bark.
People looked in shock
at the sound she made.

I felt something break.

monster

Abomination, (*English*) rendering of הָבֵעֹת (to'evah; *Hebrew*)
Adhfhuafaireacht (*Irish*) from Adúath: Great dread, monster, horror.

I twisted prayers and shat on grace
      I shunned the bread and wine and laced
the eucharist with wrath.

      I farted as I genuflected
expelling what my gut rejected.
      I lifted up my eyes.

      Will any recognise my
perfidy? Or listen to this air,
      my crooked psalmody?

I licked the clay-made feet of saints, scratched
      my name on their pale faces with my
sharpened nails. I broke the rails.

      I prowled around the altar,
opened up the holy box and
      spat into the golden space it offered.

God didn't care. I hear
      he says he's glad when
devils turn to accusation.

      I wonder if he'd wondered where I'd been.
So see me now you fucker. Here's my chance to
      lift the lid on all your people said and did.

You made me, so I stare you down. You changed me
      so I charge you now. I have been ashamed.
I bear witness now.

      I moon the crucifixion, dropping knickers round
my combat boots. My tutu and my vest
      are bulletproof. I know that people stare.

I rip my nipples from my hairy chest. A
            milkless offering. I tune my radio to noise
and turn the volume loud.

            I try to drown out all the voices from
the lips I didn't kiss, the horns I didn't break,
            the hides I didn't take

for want of purity.
            I take a piss to bless the ground. I open
all the doors. I growl God down.

Grace

Some people love it.
I despise it.

Goodness Undeserved, they
chime, but I reject the category.

Who chooses the
deserving?

Who measures?
Who is auditor of such economies?
Who maintains the ledger?

I fail every day, I know this
and what I need is mercy.

I won't take help that's proffered
if it's offered with a toxic glaze.

Fuck your grace. Forgive me.

Liquorice, Mint and Seasalt

I bought the scarf and wrapped it
round my neck. Soft wool,
speckled autumn.
Even I could see it made me
look like me.

When I showed it to you, you
took it from me,
closed your eyes and smelt it, said it
smelt of me already:
liquorice, mint and seasalt.

Eyes still shut you inhaled a little deeper
wrapped it round you,
smiled that smile you smile
inviting me to kiss you.

Discipline

The thing about violence
is how violent it is. For
some it's just the thought but
not the thud. For me, it's

bruises touched with
kindness I wish I'd
felt from others.

When I was barely grown
I saw a small boy beaten
dizzy by his daddy
for *crying like a baby.*

Then I saw the father's shock
when I saw he saw I saw.

I vomited all morning.

Magpie

You steal breath from friends.

Once I heard you gasp my gasp of cumming. Once
I heard you whisper to my son that you're his father.

Once I heard my weeping in your throat,
then you sang my song back to me, lulling me
into your sleep, the one that you took from me.

I won't forgive your trespass. I won't forget.
I remember every time I let you make me shake.

~~(And the fear in me makes the fear in me seem
bigger; makes the cupboards bare; makes mistakes
mistakes; takes and shakes and breaks.)~~

You can be your judge and thief and jury. I will nurse
my sorrow to a nipple. I'll drink from the source.

The One Thing

There must have been some other me, who
lived some other time, who realised he
knew the one thing that would save me.

And he must have found a little window,
opened it — and shouted through it —
that saving sound that saved me.

And he must have felt a failure, I am sure,
that other me, because he failed, he did, he didn't
save me from the other things that beat me.

And he must have sat, like some sad god
from sadder scriptures, and wept at all
he failed to do, he had so little time. And

all my life, I have been climbing up to little
windows — opening them — and saying
the one thing I can say: thank you.

Who, for Us Men and Our Salvation

For Sarah Williamson and Philippa Jordan

You drink whiskey during poker nights, wear
shirts your grandad wore, display the ink that's on

your unshaved chest and sign your texts to me
with x's. You drink coffee from a little glass

after early morning yoga class. You podcast
authenticity and live in parts of the city that

others have disdained. You disdain disdain.
You oil your beard. You wear 1930s shoes

bought for a small fortune in a place you say
your grandad would have loved. Like him, you believe

a woman's place is not behind the pulpit: let her
lecture in literature; let her explore the stars;

let her drink; let her work; but do not let her speak
the verb of God in public. Let her mostly be.

How to ~~Belong~~ Be Alone

It all begins with knowing nothing lasts forever,
so you might as well start packing now.

In the meantime,
practice being alive.

There will be a party where you'll feel like
nobody's paying you attention.

And there will be a party
where attention's all you'll get.

What you need to do is to remember
to talk to yourself between these parties.

And, again, there will be a day — a decade —
where you won't fit in with your body

even though you're in
the only body you're in.

You need to control your habit of forgetting
to breathe.

Remember when you were younger
and you practiced kissing on your arm?

You were on to something then.
Sometimes harm knows its own healing.

Comfort knows its own intelligence.
Kindness too. It needs no reason.

There is a you telling you another story of you.
Listen to her.

Where do you feel anxiety in your body?
The chest? The fist? The dream before waking?

The head that feels like it's at the top of the swing
or the clutch of gut like falling

& falling & falling and falling? It knows something:
you're dying. Try to stay alive.

For now, touch yourself.
I'm serious.

Touch your self. Take your hand and place your hand
some place upon your body.

And listen to the community of madness that you are.
You are such an interesting conversation.

You belong.
Here.

Abomination

Forgiveness? You can take it if you want it.
Most days I practice forgetting the hold you once
had on me. Mostly it works, most days.

There is a cave I got to once,
while shaking in a corner of your chapel.
When I found myself there, I forgot I was in your lair.

The cave came to me, and with me. I make my way there
from time to time. It comes with no demand. I enter
through the gate that has a sign that once said danger,

now says home.

May their Children's Heads be Dashed Against the Rocks

I swear, all my life I've needed
         violence and prayer.

And in order to survive this little hell,
         some necessary sadness.
                  Carrying it. Causing it as well.

So in strange gratitude, I turn to you,

— O Breaker Of A Universe Or Two
         O Silence At The Heart Of The Terrifying Question
                  O Shaper Of The Fundamental Flaw —

with undeserved respect. For all you
         saw and didn't do. For all you
                  never said. For all that you did not make new.

Notes

The first time I was told I had a devil in me, I was thirteen. A few years later, again. At eighteen I underwent three exorcisms for getting rid of the devil in me [in some ways, they were considered mild] and then had some years of [what calls itself] reparative therapy. All of this was a long time ago now. I deliberately forgot about it for a while. A long while. Almost twenty years after the first exorcism, I finally began to think about what poetry could offer.

Reparative therapies — whether offered formally, or tacitly through [what calls itself] *healing prayer*, or support for *unwanted same sex attractions* — have come under scrutiny in recent years. Legislation will ban what is already considered unacceptable by most professional psychotherapeutic associations and some religious bodies. However, it is what happens in the corners [in the underneath] that concerns me. The insidious language sneaks in [like a snake]. It takes years to leave.

I kept secrets for years. I didn't realise it was possible to imagine. I'd sought freedom in safety, not rage. Anger was salvation, so was poetry, scholarship, relief and creativity. These poems were hard-won. I'm glad I survived [many didn't]. I meet strangers everywhere who tell me about their [so-called] therapies and exorcisms. We recognise each other — by our beasts, our hunger.

Acknowledgements

These poems have been read, pored over, changed and edited, sometimes sliced in half. Often they've fought back. Thank you to those who've given time, feedback, attention, protest and pressure to these poems: Raymond Antrobus, Pat Bennett, Matt Bevis, Sophie Cabot Black, Jamie Byng, Mark Conway, Paul Doran, Nick Flynn, Vievee Francis, Greg Fromholz, Chris Fry, Cary Gibson, Lorna Goodison, Phil Harrison, Robert Heaney, Marie Howe, Major Jackson, Dave Laverty, Rachel Mann, Donna Masini, Mícheál McCann, Gail McConnell, Scott MacDougal, Brad Aaron Modlin, David Naimon, Victoria Redel, Spencer Reece, No'u Revilla, Ben Roberts, Martha Sprackland, Michael Symmons Roberts, Krista Tippett, Sam Tongue, Heather Walton, Christian Wiman, Alex Wimberly. Mo bhuíochas, agus grá ó chroí, a chairde.

Some of these poems were published, in previous versions, in: *Cat Flap; Cream City Review; Post Road; Dumbo Feather; Quarter After Eight;* and by *Desperate Literature* for the *Unamuno Festival* anthology. My thanks to the editors and teams at these publications for their dedication to poetry, and their acceptance of these poems.

Thank you to my agent, Clare Conville, and all at C&W Agency; thank you to Anya Backlund and all at Blue Flower Arts.

Thank you to Aaron Kent and everyone at Broken Sleep Books for stirring up the unrest.

Thank you to Joelle Taylor and Jericho Brown for their very kind endorsements of this hungry beast of a book.

The epigraph on page 11 is from Patrick Kavanagh's poem 'Lough Derg' and found, among many other places, in "Patrick Kavanagh: Collected Poems" published in 2005 by Penguin, edited by Antoinette Quinn.

The epigraph on page 18 is from No'u Revilla's poem: 'When you say "protestors" instead of "protectors"' from her collection "Ask the Brindled" published by Milkweed Editions in 2022.

The erasure poem "There is a Time to Love and a Time to Hate; a Time for Making War " uses excerpts of the "Responsum of the Congregation for the Doctrine of the Faith to a dubium regarding the blessing of the unions of persons of the same sex" which was published in English on the Vatican website on the 15th of March 2021.

The epigraph from Marie Howe on page 29 is from the poem "Magdalene—Seven Devils" in the collection "Magdalene", published by W.W. Norton in 2017.

FEED YOUR UNREST